A Window
to Heaven

A Window to Heaven

When Children See Life in Death

DIANE M. KOMP, M.D.

foreword by Dr. Paul Brand

ZondervanPublishingHouse

Grand Rapids, Michigan

A Division of HarperCollins*Publishers*

Let not your heart be troubled:
ye believe in God, believe also
in me. . . . I go to prepare a place
for you. And if I go and prepare a
place for you, I will come again, and
receive you unto myself; that where
I am, there ye may be also.

John 14:1–3, (KJV)

To my patients: "I love these
little people; and it is not a
slight thing when they, who are so
fresh from God, love us."

Charles Dickens, *The Old Curiosity Shop*

Contents

Acknowledgments

Parts of this book were published by the author in a series of essays in *Theology Today*, entitled "Hearts Untroubled," copyright 1988 by Diane M. Komp; "The Apple Doll House: Lessons from the Handicapped," copyright 1989 by Diane M. Komp. Portions appeared in German under the title, *Fenster in dem Himmel: Wie Kinder im Tod das Leben sehen,* copyright 1990 Aussaat Verlag for German translation only.

Foreword

This book may seem small, but it carries a powerful punch. When I first read the manuscript, I was so impressed that I wrote to Dr. Diane Komp and told her that what she had to say deserved a larger book and a fuller treatment. She replied that she was "reluctant to pad it and stretch the good stuff thin," and, of course, she is right.

The "punch" that this book delivers is powerful because it comes out of the personal experience of a specialist in childhood cancer. One does not become professor of pediatrics at Yale University without being at the head of one's profession. And yet Dr. Komp has chosen to specialize in pediatric oncology, which means that, however well she does her job, a high proportion of her patients are going to be little children who will die of cancer.

Her experience belies conventional wisdom which says that it is easy to believe in a loving God so long as all goes well. People who experience pain, sickness, and death at close quarters often find themselves moving closer to God rather than away from him. This is the tension at the heart of the biblical story of Job. Before the court of God, Satan asserts that the reason Job is such an upright and God-fearing man is that he has been blessed with fine children and a prosperous business. He then adds, in effect, "Take away his wealth and let his children die, let me destroy his health, introduce real suffering into his life, and then see what happens to his faith in God." Likewise, many people feel that the single most powerful argument against the reality of the love of God is that innocent little children suffer and die.

To answer such a claim, we simply have to read this book. We discover that when Diane Komp started her career as a pediatric cancer specialist, she described herself as somewhere between agnostic and atheist. Then we witness how, through her experiences at the bedside of many dying children, she returned to a belief in God and recognized the reality of God's love.

I have two reasons why I want to urge people to read this book. One is that there are a lot of people whose faith really is dependent on things going well. These people need to be introduced to real life as it has been experienced by a thoughtful person of integrity, who has been constantly exposed to suffering and death in little children.

The other reason is professional. As a physician myself, I have loved my profession and have observed its evolution over almost fifty years. I am distressed by some of the profound changes that I have seen and by the widening gap between doctors and patients. Physicians, surgeons, and medical students need to hear the message of this book. The current generation of doctors is encouraged to keep a distance between themselves and their patients; they are advised to avoid becoming involved with their patients' feelings. There is a move afoot to stop using the word *patient*, with its past image of a caring personal relationship, and to call the people we care for *clients*. A doctor today is seen as selling a service to a client. The physician-patient relationship is becoming a business transaction.

One reason for this trend is that the technology of medicine has become much more efficient. Diagnosis has been made easier through laboratory tests, magnetic resonance imaging scans, and computer analysis of health questionnaires filled in by patients. Personal contact seems almost unnecessary. Recording a medical history and performing a full physical examination takes time. If one allows a patient to discuss fears and hopes, it takes even more time—time that could be better spent seeing more clients and increasing revenue.

Whatever the cause, the fact remains that few of today's doctors are trained to develop personal rapport with these "clients," and many are embarrassed to be faced with questions that relate to personal fears or to family and social reactions that often accompany serious illness or impending death. The author herself was advised to avoid developing personal feelings for her patients. "Just do your job."

Dr. Diane Komp does not enter into a theoretical discussion of these matters, but teaches by example. She allows us to observe her own reactions as she looks back at her early attempts to help her young patients. She discovered very early that there was no way in which she could treat chronic illness in children without getting to know them. And she found that to know them is often to love them. To love a child who will soon die is to expose oneself to the pain of dying. To talk with the parents afterward is to share in their bereavement.

In this book we meet an unusual doctor. Dr. Komp insists on making house calls and tries to be present at times of crisis. She asks to be informed if one of her children shows signs of impending death; because she wants to be there, for the sake of the child and for the sake of the parents and—it soon became clear to this doctor—for her own sake. She found that she wanted the reinforcement to her own faith that comes from seeing these little ones return to their Lord in the natural way of a child to its Parent.

My own first appointment after graduating as a doctor was as resident surgical officer at the Hospital for Sick Children in London, England. I saw many little children die and it often fell to me to break the news to parents and family. I tried to behave with professional dignity and demonstrate sympathy while I answered questions. Later, after I went to India to teach surgery, one of my first patients was the baby daughter of a Christian missionary couple. After I struggled to keep her alive, little Anne died. I have never felt such an utter failure as when I handed the tiny body over to her parents. When I followed the funeral procession, I cried, almost as though it had been my own child.

More than thirty years later I met with that family again, this time with the grown brothers and sisters of the little one who had died. I found that they had no memory of a surgeon who had failed. They all treasured the memory, or at least the oft repeated story, of a surgeon who had cared for Anne and who wept with them when she died. By involving himself in their crisis, he had helped to turn it all into a positive experience.

I learned late what Diane Komp learned early: Little children do not quickly lose the sense of where they're from, nor do they fear where they're going. Fear is often introduced into the process of dying by the very technology and hospital environment meant to help. It is the special privilege of the dedicated physician to be a human interface that facilitates peace and preserves hearts untroubled.

Dr. Paul Brand
Seattle, Washington
December 1991

Author's Preface

I had intended to wait until retirement before I committed these stories to the printed page. There were snippets stored in my computer's memory plus assorted anecdotes committed to paper placemats from assorted diners (when inspiration came at an odd moment). Organizing all this seemed a suitable project to keep me out of mischief when it was time for younger clinicians to carry the beeper and fill out the insurance forms.

The time frame was changed by the insistence of my pastor, Ken Norris. Over the years, I had used a number of these stories in our own church to illustrate sermons, enliven adult education programs, or even punctuate conversation. One particular Sunday I told a congregation who had assumed that I had always been a Christian the story of my spiritual journey. Ken said, "You've got to start writing about this. The way you tell the story, it could even convince unbelieving clergy."

Somehow I had been naive enough to think that

unbelieving scientists were the toughest to reach. Ken's words persuaded me to consider publication at an earlier date, so it is the Rev. Dr. Kendrick Norris who is the first person whom I must acknowledge with gratitude and tell he was right.

I thrashed around on the keyboard for a long time before I had a first draft of an essay that I was even willing to consider. This is astonishing since in my long career of scientific writing, I rarely exceed a single draft, even for manuscripts that would be published in the *New England Journal of Medicine*. What I am writing here I consider more important than any editorial I have produced for that august journal. I chose to launch my essays in *Theology Today* (which I consider to be the theological equivalent of the *New England Journal of Medicine*) after reading an editorial by the senior editor, Hugh Kerr, about theological writing and the philosophy of that journal. He seemed to be a man of intellect, courage, and imagination. His prompt response included a copy of the memorial service program for one of his best friends' grandson. This boy, stricken with leukemia, had experienced similar visions to those of the children described in this book. I cannot adequately express my gratitude to "Tim" Kerr for his continuing friendship and support. It was he who finally said, "Di, it's time for the book."

Special thanks must also be offered to Paul and Gladys Minear, Fr. William and Deacon Anne Beasley, Leanne Payne, Elke and Roland Werner, and countless other friends and colleagues who supported me while this manuscript has been in preparation. Finally, I must thank Dr. Paul Brand, Philip Yancey, and the staff of Zondervan, including Lyn Cryderman and Scott Bolinder who are responsible for the book reaching an English speaking readership in this edition.

A word is in order about the content. I have never felt that these stories belong to me. Rather, they were given to me as gifts, and I have tried to be a good steward of those treasures. To maximize accuracy, I consulted with the children's parents whenever possible and appropriate. In many cases, my relationship with these remarkable people has been strengthened by the telling of their children's stories. To protect privacy, it was often wise to change names and minor details. In some cases, I have changed the names back from the pseudonyms at the request of the parents.

Finally, this book deals primarily with spiritual experiences surrounding death. Today, at least 50 percent of children with cancer survive and some of them and their parents will be reading this book. These "survivors" are the special brothers and sisters to the children who are now in the care of their heavenly Parent. They and I are concerned that by focusing on stories of children who died, you, the reader, may think of cancer as an automatic death sentence. Nothing is farther from the truth. Today the majority of children who experience cancer will outlive that diagnosis. One of the most important young people in the preparation of this book is a twelve-year-old girl with bone cancer who is looking forward to surgery that will save her affected leg. We expect her to remain disease free with the help of chemotherapy. She was not afraid to read about other children with cancer who faced and experienced death, even when she had every right to be hopeful and optimistic. Korey and I would like to share with you a quotation from one of my best friends who died from cancer one year ago today: "For the Christian, the Big C is not cancer; the Big C is Christ."

Diane M. Komp, M. D.
New Haven, Ct.
December 17, 1991

—— Prologue ——

Journey to Disbelief

> With three or more people there is something bold in the air: direct things get said which would frighten two people alone. . . . To be three is to be in public, you feel safe.
>
> Elizabeth Bowen, *The House in Paris*

*L*ast year I shared a compartment on a railroad train to Frankfurt with an elderly German widow and a Greek auto mechanic. Busy knitting needles punctuated the widow's story as she told of her anticipated visit to her beloved grandchildren. The Greek gentleman was revisiting the village where he had learned his professional trade years earlier. Both of my fellow passengers were curious about a German-speaking American.

When I told them that I had traveled to Marburg to meet with a group of medical students who wanted to discuss the relevance of faith to the practice of medicine, they stared at me in disbelief. Surely they had misunderstood me. Perhaps my German wasn't as fluent as it initially sounded. To them, I looked and acted nothing like their image of a professor of medicine. They were sure, however, that I was American. What other genre of middle-aged female would board a train in Germany dressed in blue jeans and Nike sneakers? Perhaps I wasn't talking about *German* medical students. One hears all sorts of things about the religiosity of Americans.

But they had heard me correctly.

The animated Greek groped for words in a language he hadn't used for thirty years: "The only verse in the Bible that our Greek doctors know is about the thirty pieces of silver. But they've raised the price. They'd hardly settle for that low a fee anymore. Why the chiropractor in our village only charges you the most you can afford to pay!" I resisted the temptation to ask him how he set his fees in his auto service station.

The widow's concerns were more profound: "Our doctors in Germany don't believe in God" was her sad opinion. "When my husband was dying of cancer, I asked our family practitioner if he believed in God. He said no. I asked him how he could help someone to die if he did not believe himself. He just looked away."

❧ ❧ ❧

This German family doctor reminded me of Albert Camus's fictional French physician, Dr. Rieux. In *The Plague*, Rieux worked tirelessly and compassionately fighting against an absurd situation (bubonic plague) for which to him at least, there was no higher explanation, only a biological reality. In attending to a friend on his deathbed, the doctor,

... could only stand, unavailing, on the shore, empty-handed and sick at heart, unarmed and helpless yet again under the onset of calamity. And thus, when the end came, the tears that blinded Rieux's eyes were tears of impotence; and he did not see Tarrou roll over, face to the wall and die. . . . The doctor could not tell if Tarrou had found peace, now that it was over, but for himself he had a feeling that no peace was possible to him henceforth, any more than there can be an armistice for a mother bereaved of her son or for a man who buries his friend.[1]

The German and Greek practitioners that my fellow passengers encountered are typical of the average Western physician. Although I know physicians of deep personal faith both in Europe and in America, they are the minority.

Like the fictional Rieux, most doctors working in a medically privileged society feel unfruitful when our efforts fail and the disease is not cured. These feelings of powerlessness not only negatively affect how doctors interpret their discipline but also how they approach the human beings they attend at the bedside.

For many young doctors who begin their careers from a perspective of faith in God, the path of medical education becomes a journey to disbelief. When I started my career as a pediatric cancer specialist, I vacillated between being an agnostic and an atheist—though I spent little time considering exactly where my beliefs fit. Like many of my fellow students, I sought the help of my professors for career guidance, and they were most willing to offer what advice they could from their own experience.

When I was faced with my first patient who would die (a young woman my own age with end-stage kidney disease), I asked my clinical mentor how we as young doctors were supposed to deal with our feelings about so-called "innocent suffering." He responded that the answer was *not* to attempt to deal with feelings, simply to do our work and concentrate on that. Hard work, he said, is a good tonic for untamed and uneasy feelings. His advice seemed good because it appeared to help me through the ordeal.

I learned from him to keep my feelings about patients as numb as possible. One of the side effects of this approach was that my faith began to slip away with each passing child.

Over the years I have come to the conclusion that dramatic conversion to disbelief is rare. More often, faith dies from disuse atrophy, a failure to be exercised. Such was my experience. I settled for an ersatz-existentialist's resolution and decided not to attempt to find a meaning in suffering. I only sought to fight against it.

ॐ ॐ ॐ

A recent study reveals that few American medical students find anything in their educational process to support and sustain the idealism with which they began their studies. Something about the educational process robs them of their original passion for service and substitutes a different, more self-oriented motivation. A young person who previously identified with the sufferer moves to a position where there is a seemingly unbridgeable distance between patient and physician.

The chaplain of a medical school interviewed clinical faculty members to determine how these experienced physicians coped with the extraordinary stresses of their work. He quotes an internist who is representative of his colleagues in his description of how he has learned to cope with the absurdity of serious illness: "I no longer assume the responsibility for the successful outcome or failure, if the success or failure is determined by the impotency of medicine as opposed to my mistake. I do not establish friendships with my patients; there is no socializing. I learned that very early on."[2]

Thus, my own story is not the only one of a physician whose early idealistic and religious convictions were to be derailed during medical education. However, the journey begins but does not end in derailment.

1

A Choir of Angels

*For he shall give his angels charge
over thee, to keep thee in all thy
ways. They shall bear thee up in
their hands.*

Psalm 91:11–12 (KJV)

*M*y strategy of remaining emotionally detached from my patients simply did not work. Taking care of children is quite different from treating adults. Internists and surgeons may get away with keeping their distance, but for a pediatrician treating children with chronic diseases, it was not a viable option. Whether atheists, agnostics, or firm believers, pediatricians must learn to listen to our young patients if we would gain their cooperation and practice something more communicative than veterinary medicine.

One of the bitter-sweet privileges of caring for children with cancer is that you grow to love them and bask in that love returned. This love returned is a form of love that is rarely seen on this earth. It is unconditional. Part of that love entails, on occasion, to share the road toward death.

As a young "post-Christian" doctor, I did not pretend to have any handy theological solutions to people's existential dilemmas, but I could be a friend on the way. Many times I listened politely to parents who groped for God in their most painful hour. I respected them all for their journeys but I heard no convincing evidence in their revelations to challenge my way of thinking. If I were to believe, I always assumed, it would require the testimony of reliable witnesses without culturally determined expectations about death or without I-can't-afford-not-to-believe views of a hereafter.

꙳ ꙳ ꙳

In the early 1970s, brave parents helped me, a young oncologist at the time, implement a home death program in a rural area of the South. I have visited children at home who experienced physical pain, but I have never seen a child at home experience fear. In their homes, I was the guest and they were clearly the hosts. Children accurately reported their medical condition in this environment, since they felt in control. With encouragement and support, many families found that pain and other dreaded complications of terminal cancer could be managed. If the children did need hospitalization for comfort, they themselves felt free to suggest it. If they preferred to die at home, we made it possible long before hospice services were more generally available.[3]

In their homes, children would ceremoniously wipe the dust from my black doctor's bag and swear that they would not report me to the American Medical Association for making house calls.[4] My young patients and I would discuss what type of examination was appropriate, what tests might be useful, and they themselves determined the limits. The syringes, needles, and blood test tubes in my bag were rarely employed. The visit to the child's room was followed by tea in the kitchen with the rest of the family. Special attention to the brothers and sisters was required since those who would continue to live also needed care.

Most children who die do not pass from this life without prior clinical warning signals. Often parents of children at home or nursing staff of hospitalized patients could alert me in time to be at the bedside for that moment. The first time I sat by a child dying of cancer, I sat at her bed from a concept of duty rather than in anticipation of joy.

🐸 🐸 🐸

Today many children with leukemia are cured, but this was not the case when Anna first became sick.[5] Her therapy brought her periods of time when she was disease-free over the five years she received treatment, but she faced the end of her life at age seven. Before she died, she mustered the final energy to sit up in her hospital bed and say: "The angels—they're so beautiful! Mommy, can you see them? Do you hear their singing? I've never heard such beautiful singing!" Then she laid back on her pillow and died.

Her parents reacted as if they had been given the most precious gift in the world. The hospital chaplain in attendance was more comfortable with the psychological than with the spiritual and he beat a hasty retreat to leave the existentialist doctor alone with the grieving family. Together we contemplated a spiritual mystery that transcended our understanding and experience. For weeks to follow the thought that stuck in my head was: Have I found a reliable witness?

Every time I hear the angel prologue to Boito's opera *Mephistopheles*, I think of Anna and the other "angels" who brought their oncologist back to the life of faith. Because of these children, my life has been changed and I have seen other lives changed. Stalled journeys of faith have been resumed. This book is written as a witness to these children and their parents, just as they have been faithful witnesses to me.

❧ ❧ ❧

Several years ago, I had the opportunity to tell the story of Anna and her vision of angels at a church conference. One participant was particularly overcome by the story and ran out of the room in tears. His reaction seemed to be a very personal one rather than generalized sadness about death in children. Later in the day, he returned and explained to the group why he was so profoundly affected by Anna's story.

Twenty years before, Walter had personally witnessed a tragic accident. A beer truck was parked on an incline adjacent to a local pub while the driver made his delivery. The brakes of the truck were somehow faulty.

Just as Walter walked out the barroom door and reached the street, the truck began to move unattended. It accelerated down a steep hill toward a mother and young child.

Walter anticipated that the child would be pinned against a wall if the truck was not stopped. He tried to catch it in time to put on the emergency brake. His efforts failed, in part, because his reflexes were impeded by the large amount of alcohol in his system. In fact, he was by that time an established alcoholic.

His worst fears were realized and the child was fatally mutilated. In his alcoholic stupor, he thought he saw the child's head surrounded by light and heard her last words to her mother: "Don't worry, Mommy, I'll be okay."

The shock and guilt he felt and his sense of a supernatural presence at the moment of her death precipitated a two-week drinking binge but also served, finally, to lead him to seek effective help for his alcoholism.

Can there be anything good about the death of a child?

As Walter told his story, I remembered a comment that he had made earlier in the group's discussion—a comment that had led me to tell Anna's story to begin with. Walter said something to the effect that children are important in God's redemptive plan for us.

His reflection is consistent with the words of Jesus who often pointed to children when he required an apt metaphor for the kingdom of heaven. Jesus rarely used adults as role models for spiritual maturity.

Like Walter, I must ask myself what my life would be like today if I were not privileged to know these dying children. Would I have found that virtuous window that later defined the most important content of my life?

2

Hearts Unsure, Hearts Untroubled

To have his path made clear for him is the aspiration of every human being in our beclouded and tempestuous existence.

Joseph Conrad, *The Mirror of the Sea*

I cannot report that the choir of angels resulted in a dramatic conversion experience for me or in an instant adoption of the traditional beliefs that I had abandoned. For me it was a prologue. The experience posed the important questions and hinted at the answers that might follow.

A prologue tunes our ears to the composer's desired cadences and relegates former dominating themes to less active memory. My heart remained unsure when I left Anna's hospital room, but my ear was definitely retuned.

Although physicians do not generally recognize it, our ears are regularly retuned. We pride ourselves in being objective and complete in our observations, in hearing and telling the whole story. The fact is that as long as it is a human listener who is recording the facts, the "truth" is filtered through personal experience. If a "fact" does not make sense to us, we may not even hear it. Once I caught this cadence of old familiar truth, I realized that, in my acquired "deafness," I might not know everything about my patients that was important to know. With the retuning of my ear, I became a more objective, less censoring listener.

My introduction to Mary Beth came somewhat later. She was six years old when she was diagnosed with cancer. After a brief period out of the hospital, her disease recurred. In deference to her parents' wishes, her worsening condition was not discussed in her presence. The change in treatment meant that Mary Beth would need to be admitted to the hospital shortly before Christmas. She wasn't afraid of the hospital because she had made friends with the nurses on the pediatric ward at the time of her first admission. A holiday party was planned for the children, and Mary Beth's favorite nurse bought her a red velvet dress to wear. Mysteriously, the child refused to wear it for reasons she firmly declined to discuss. Mary Beth was fond of pretty dresses and so her behavior was very much out of character.

After she completed her treatment, her blood counts indicated that she was not responding. The child's poor prognosis was discussed with her family, and Mary Beth was discharged to come back to visit as an outpatient.

At the time of a return visit, her mother confessed to being baffled by a dream that the child shared with her. She asked me what I thought it meant. Mary Beth told her mother that Jesus came to her in a dream with one of her grandfathers who had died before she was born. Together, Jesus and her grandfather told her of her impending death and encouraged her not to be afraid. She awoke with the peace and reassurance that she would soon be with Jesus and her grandfather.

She had never met that grandfather but recognized him from family photographs. It was her absolute peace that baffled her mother. Mary Beth died at home on Christmas Eve and was dressed in her new red velvet dress when at the funeral her brief life was finally celebrated.

Although her mother was baffled by the dream, my previous experience with Anna and other children had opened a window for me that had long been tightly shuttered. I recognized a pattern in their stories that helped me re-examine systems of belief that lay on the other side of the window.

The stories I have witnessed and am now sharing with you are not based on the type of systematic research that makes scientists feel comfortable and secure. At the same time, being comfy and certain does not necessarily mean that we know all the truth.

Scientists tend to define what we are trying to understand in terms that we already know. This increases our comfort level. We are cautious by temperament. We are reluctant to speak out on any subject until we are certain of it. We hesitate to speak about nonscience in a manner that might be misinterpreted as an *ex cathedra* scientific report. We do not know what to do with observations that fall outside our own carefully controlled experiments. When we cannot speak the language of science, we would rather remain mute.

For many years, I did not share in public these stories of the children, but I was nurtured by them privately. *Los Angeles Times* journalist Dianne Klein captures this reluctance when she quotes one of my colleagues who has shared similar experiences: "Talking about this with me makes [Dr.] Geni Bennetts a little uncomfortable. She doesn't want to sound like a kook, which she is most certainly not. 'I cannot accept it as science. I accept it as part of life. I have never tried to prove it—or disprove it. I just accept it.'"[6]

🐸 🐸 🐸

The children's experiences did not correspond with anything I learned in medical school, but they did remind me of the words of Jesus that I learned in my youth that are recorded in the gospel of John. These words were meant to dispel the fear and sadness Jesus saw on his disciples' faces in the garden of Gethsemane:

> Let not your heart be troubled: ye believe in God, believe also in me. In my Father's house are many mansions: if it were not so, I would have told you. I go to prepare a place for you. And if I go and prepare a place for you, I will come again, and receive you unto myself; that where I am, there ye may be also" (John 14:1–3, KJV).

Jesus spoke of an alternative to the unsure, uncertain heart—the heart untroubled. The untroubled heart that he describes is not achieved by having access to more information about the feared subject. Neither is it the result of an intellectual desensitization to painful words and concepts. Theologian Paul Minear interprets this peace simply as a gift:

> The peace is not a vague state of bliss in general, but *his* peace, something belonging to him that he alone can give as a farewell bequest. Nor is it spread on the winds for universal appreciation; it is given only to *his own*, those who belong to him and who are being commissioned to carry on his work. It forever links their work to his, their story to his.[7]

The stories in this book link an ancient story with the children's stories. Rather than medical case reports based on the certainty of what scientists currently understand, they are simply an attempt to be faithful to what I have heard. In this sense, they continue Jesus' commissioned work of revealing that there is a realm that we cannot yet fully understand. The greatest gift in my life has been in linking the ancient story and the children's stories to my own. In accepting the linkage, God has ministered to my unsure heart with the gift of hearts untroubled.

3

Something Better Than Near Death

*To die is different from what any
one supposed.*

Walt Whitman, *Leaves of Grass*

*S*ince I first began publicly to tell these children's remarkable stories, some have linked my work with what has been described as the "near-death experience." Although the reported near-death experiences bear some superficial similarities to some aspects of these stories of children who would soon die, there are also striking differences.

Most near-death stories involve adults who are afraid to tell their experiences to anyone for fear that they will not be believed. The young children who experience these visions, however, never question that they will be believed. Unlike the adults whom they tell, the children share their stories without a trace of reticence.

If I could use one word to summarize the adult experiences it would be *Aha!* A more apropos summary word for the children would be *Amen*.

For adults, the experience is often spiritually *revolutionary*, a type of conversion experience that puts them on a new road. For children, however, the experience is more spiritually *evolutionary*, progress on an already familiar pathway.

The adults frequently report vague spiritual beings, but the children are often more specific, naming Jesus or describing angels. Dr. Geni Bennetts tells this story:

> Another boy, a 4 year old Asian whose family did not practice a Christian faith, had a vision of an angel visiting him and then summoned members of the hospital staff into his room. He thanked each of them for helping him and then said goodbye. Then he laid down and died. . . . He was not upset, not at all. But you can imagine. There wasn't a dry eye on the floor.[8]

Young children sick with advanced cancer are similar to adults in reporting peaceful feelings or seeing light. I have never heard a young child suffering from cancer report seeing a tunnel or darkness, feeling they were "out-of-body," or having a review of life events. These are common components of near-death experiences in adults.

Many of the reports from adults take place in the setting of clinical death, coma, or another form of brain impairment. The children I am describing report experiences in dreams, visions, or prayer and are infrequently brain dysfunctional at the time.[9]

❧ ❧ ❧

Developmental psychologists would have us believe that children are less complete than adults and need experience to inform them about the way the world really is. Yet Jesus tells us that we should be like them, these little ones "fresh from God," if we would even begin to understand his Father's love.

Henri Nouwen offers his understanding of how God's love is revealed in Christ:

> How is that love [of God] made visible through Jesus? It is made visible in the descending way. That is the great mystery of the Incarnation. . . . In the gospel it's quite obvious that Jesus chose . . . it not once but over and over again. At each critical moment he deliberately sought the way downwards.[10]

❧ ❧ ❧

The closest story to the adult near-death experience that I can recall from my own practice involved a young adult whose cancer began when he was in high school. Tom was nineteen years old when his cancer recurred, but he refused to accept the relapse as a death sentence.

He declined further chemotherapy because there was no promise of cure even if he endured the side effects, but he still believed that he would find a way to be healed of cancer, to become an "exceptional cancer patient." His parents considered taking him to court to be declared mentally incompetent.

While he was in the hospital, the tumor in his cervical spinal cord advanced to the point where he became quadriplegic. Although he could neither walk nor lift his arms, he still would not believe that he was going to die from his disease, and he worried whether permitting such "negative thoughts" would interfere with "positive healing thoughts."

In this condition he was discharged to his home on his twentieth birthday. When I visited him, he was able to move only his head and neck and required total nursing care. When we were alone, he told me of a vision that came to him while he was meditating.

Tom saw himself in a beautiful garden and saw a man there, seated on a bench. The man's fingers were like roses, and he walked with Tom in the garden and talked to him. The man touched him, and Tom reported that he moved in his bed for the first time in months. He did not want to leave the garden or the man's presence, but his companion went ahead and told him that he could not come with him yet.

I asked Tom if he knew who the man was. He said, "I *know* it was Jesus."

I could tell from his eyes that he was afraid that I would not believe him. Thinking of the images he described, I thought for sure that he must be recreating the old gospel hymn "In the Garden."

I come to the garden alone,
While the dew is still on the roses.
And the voice I hear, falling on my ear,
The Son of God discloses.

And He walks with me and He talks with me,
And He tells me I am His own;

And the joy we share as we tarry there,
None other has ever known.

He speaks and the sound of His voice
Is so sweet the birds hush their singing.
And the melody that He gave to me,
Within my heart is ringing.

I'd stay in the garden with Him
Though the night around me be falling
But He bids me go, through the voice of woe,
His voice to me is calling.[11]

Tom was confused by my question, because he had never heard of the hymn. When I sang it for him, he did not recognize the melody but was excited because he recognized in the words the parallel image to his vision. Two days later, he told his parents that he would not live through the night and died peacefully in his sleep.

As I sit by the beds of these children, I have seen God's love made manifest in this descending way. I have seen Jesus Christ come again and again and again to bring peace and to link the children's stories with his own.

They will receive from the Father a peace that the world will be powerless to destroy. It is this peace that will give new meaning to the act of believing. Now to believe will be to rejoice at Jesus' going and coming, to love him in such a way as to share his courage, to continue his mission to the same world but without coveting the world's peace.[12]

"Peace I leave with you," says Jesus. "My peace I give to you; not as the world gives do I give to you. Let not your hearts be troubled, neither let them be afraid" (John 14:27, RSV).

4

A Mystery Story

God made man because he loves stories.

Elie Wiesel, *The Gates of the Forest*

*S*ome people delight in turning simple truths into big mysteries. I have heard it in sermons as the preacher lingers lovingly over the very enunciation of mystery. The homiletical intention is dénouement, end of argument. *Behold, I shew you a myssssss-tery!*

For medical doctors, a mystery is anything but a finale. It is more a call to action, like Teddy Roosevelt leading the charge up San Juan Hill. How we hate unsolved mysteries!

What would you think if you had a mysterious chest pain and I said, "Ah, it's a mystery!" and walked away? So doctors and others squirm in the pew when we hear sermonizing about the mystery of suffering, focusing on the symptoms but not suggesting in any way a cause or a treatment. It is, after all, the mystery of suffering rather than a "scientific view of the world" that poses the greatest stumbling block to faith for people like me.

But the ways of children are a deep mystery. Children hold the key to unlocking life's greatest mysteries.

And though it goes against their nature, pediatricians must learn to live with, and even appreciate, this mystery. Always at home with the spiritual nature of children, the Great Physician was the ideal pediatrician: "O Father, Lord of Heaven and earth, I thank you for hiding these things from the clever and intelligent and for showing them to mere children" (Matthew 11:25, PHILLIPS).

When the clever are really intelligent, they look to children for answers. For our sake, Jesus became a vulnerable child.

I was recently asked to consult on an adult patient with a rare tumor. Various caregivers recorded their concerns about his mental competence, or alluded to a demanding and arrogant attitude. His original symptom was pain and two months later that pain was only worse.

When meeting with the patient I did not find him incompetent, arrogant, or excessively demanding. But I did find him to be in pain. Despite the morphine, he was in worse pain than I have ever seen any cancer patient bear. After he started treatment with chemotherapy, the morphine dose quickly diminished. Those who once thought him to be arrogant and demanding changed their opinions. His intern reported, "He's like a little kid, he's so excited about each and every improvement."

Perhaps only a pediatrician would smile in relief that a patient could earn the privilege to be seen as a child. I hope that when it is my turn to be a patient, I am equally privileged. I hope that I will have the courage to report all the mysteries that excite me.

❧ ❧ ❧

Religious educator Sophia Cavalletti refers to a mysterious bond between God and the child. She tells of a three-year-old who grew up without religious influence and had never heard the name of God spoken. "The little one asked her father, 'Where does the world come from?' He responded with a secularized theory of the origins of the world, but added, 'However, there are those who say that all this comes from a very powerful being and they call that being God.' His daughter joyously exclaimed, 'I knew what you told me wasn't true; it is God, it is God!'"[13]

To those who care about people who suffer, the mystery can be hard to bear. It sometimes appears that God doesn't take very good care of the godly.

A pastor wrote to me of his personal struggle during his seminary days:

> I worked as a chaplain ... and was at times overwhelmed by the seeming indiscretion of suffering. Many nights I lay in bed for hours wondering if I would ever be able to inspire people to believe in God when I wasn't always sure. Rick was a teenager I got to know while I was there. He had ... cancer and more than anything it was the courage which he demonstrated that somehow gave me strength.

In his Christmas allegory, *The Story of the Other Wise Man*, Henry Van Dyke uses holy imagination to envision a godly dream that was derailed.[14] Artaban was a fourth magi meant to join the others on their trip to Bethlehem. He was detained en route, ministering to the many unfortunates he met along the way. His life's mission seemed a failure as he lay dying in a street on Easter morning and met the risen Christ. Jesus' words to Artaban (and the parents of my patients): Inasmuch as you have done this unto one of the least of these, my brethren, you have done it unto me.

One father who is a gifted story-teller wove a nightly bedtime story for his son. Ernie interrupted one story to ask, "If I die now and you and Mom don't get to heaven for a long time, will I forget you?"

"No way, son," Dad answered. "What's a long time, anyhow? Jesus died 2,000 years ago and doesn't that seem like just yesterday?"

O death where is thy sting when a loving heavenly Father coaches a human dad in the fine art of stinger-removal? A mysteriously beautiful fellowship, this fellowship of suffering.

Death stings in New Haven at my favorite vegetarian restaurant. Its walls proclaim the virtues of fiber and decry the evils of nuclear waste. They write your first name on the check at that restaurant in order to locate you when your meal is ready. Five of their waiters have spelled my name "Die" rather than "Di." Not even a popular young princess came first to their minds, only their greatest fear.

I asked one young man why he thought to spell my name that way. My question made him exceedingly nervous: "I am absolutely terrified by death. I can't even tolerate to say the word." I have never had the courage to tell him that I'm an oncologist.

Eight-year-old Jason Gaes has been through surgery, chemotherapy, and radiotherapy for lymphoma, but he does not let the risk of death from "cansur" sting. If Jason could meet my frightened vegetarians, he would tell them: "Every bodys godda die sometime. If you can find it get a poster that says Help me to remember Lord that nothing is gonna happen today that you and me can't handle together. Then hang it in your room and read it at night when your scared."[15]

Oat bran and sunflower oil may reduce the risk of disease, but they will not convert the heart and cast out fear.

One particularly discouraging day at work, I tried to cheer myself up. I said to myself, "Self, what did you do today that made you feel really good?"

And I answered myself, "I spent an hour with the parents of a child who is dying."

The fact is, some of the most peace-giving moments in my adult life have been spent with these children and their parents.

People who describe their experiences with cancer often use metaphors associated with change or conversion. One young woman without a Christian background used the term "passing from death unto life" to describe her understanding of survival of childhood Hodgkin's disease. She planned a career in medicine to fulfill her sense of being "saved for a purpose." The young people I treat for life-threatening illnesses seek a meaning in their experience.

In sharing the mystery with my patients, I find meaning for my own life. Peter Kreeft says that science only asks *what* and *how*, philosophy asks *why*, but it is religion that asks *who*. God's great mystery story is, after all, a "whodunit."[16]

Seeing, then, that we are surrounded by so great a cloud of witnesses, let us solve with patience the mystery story that is set before us.

5

Gifted Clowns

I gave this mite a gift I denied to all of you—eternal innocence. She will evoke the kindness that will keep you human. She will remind you every day that I AM WHO I AM.

Morris West, *Clowns of God*

*M*y first professional encounters with Down's syndrome were during the era when families were advised to institutionalize the mentally retarded.[17] The medical credo of the day was that family life was disrupted by the presence of a severely retarded child.[18] Thus pediatricians counseled parents to institutionalize "idiots" for the sake of the rest of the family.[19]

Leukemia and some other forms of cancer are more common in Down's syndrome children than in the population at large. But in contrast to our other patients, these children with cancer came to us not from loving homes but from sterile institutions. As I worked with these youngsters, I kept asking myself how a physician can continuously subject a child to painful procedures when no one counts the quantity or quality of added days as blessed?

In the late seventies, I moved to a new position and was confronted with a refreshingly different situation. In a community with large, closely knit families and effective support organizations, most of my

Down's syndrome patients were vibrant youngsters who lived at home. I encountered well-informed families whose retarded children knew their personal worth. These were new lessons for me to learn:

> No, it was to shame the wise that God chose what is foolish by human reckoning, and to shame what is strong that he chose what is weak by human reckoning; those whom the world thinks common and contemptible are the ones that God has chosen—those who are nothing at all to show up those who are everything (1 Corinthians 1:27–28, PHILLIPS).

Donny's family instructed me to treat him like any other child with leukemia—just as they treated him as a normal child in all possible areas of his life. During his first admission to our hospital I remember most Donny's passionate desire not to be underestimated. We did not see the frustration and anger that surely must accompany chronic underestimation. We met a charming performer with years of experience playing to dense audiences of the presumably mentally able.

His parents always did their best to help Donny reach his highest potential, but there was the rest of the world to deal with. Ruth and Bob poured out their hearts to a child psychiatrist about issues surely too profound for their retarded son to comprehend. As they talked to him, Donny stood to the side, feigning disinterest. His pretense was noted by the psychiatrist, who asked, "Donny, do people ever underestimate you?" Hand on hip, Donny shot back, "Doc, you'd better believe it!"

His mother was born in Puerto Rico to a Baptist mother and a Roman Catholic father. As a child, Ruth attended services for both each Sunday, and her own approach to religion combined the best of each. Whether it be the rich symbolism of Catholicism or the Baptist emphasis on personal faith, it was very important to her that Donny's personal religious commitment be recognized. She searched for a Christian church that would allow him to learn at his own pace. When Donny's spiritual growth rate exceeded the piety pace of the "normal," she warned priests and pastors not to hold her Donny back! The retarded child I met was more thoroughly Christian than I was.

At the time of his final relapse, chemotherapy offered him no hope of long-term remission. The family planned a visit to the grandparents who had been unable to accept this retarded grandchild. Donny climbed onto his grandmother's lap and said, "Grandma, I'm going to be with Jesus soon." His parents were astonished since no one had taught this to him.

≥ ≥ ≥

There are some basic flaws in the proposition that spiritual truth is best apprehended by the most mature, most logical, most modern, and most brilliant minds. Such intellectual chauvinism is certainly in conflict with Jesus' admonition to look to the children to find the secrets of the Kingdom: "Thou hast hidden these things from the wise and understanding and revealed them to babes" (Matthew 11:25, RSV).

After Donny's death, Ruth went to work supervising the kitchen and dining-room staff at the Apple Doll House restaurant, a regional program that employs adult retarded citizens. How many parents who lose a child have the privilege to go to work each day and see the same beloved face? Seeing Down's syndrome people each day was a miraculous way to assuage the grief and retain the wonder of the small life that was no longer part of hers. No manager could have loved her employees more than Ruth or was more gifted in affirming their worth.

One of Ruth's charges, Mary Kate, excelled as a waitress and was soon promoted to hostess. When I visited, she always served my table despite her exalted new job description. She led an active life outside of work, living in a group home with other adults with Down's syndrome and competing in a variety of sports events.

It was Christmas time when I came for lunch with three guests. While we were contemplating the excellent alternatives on the menu, Mary Kate was in the corner quietly repeating, over and over again, "Croissant, croissant, croissant." The menu was arranged by numbers to simplify things for the staff. One of my guests ordered by number, but Mary Kate was not about to have her rehearsal efforts wasted: "Would that be the ham and cheese *croissant?*"

My guest complimented her on her superb French pronunciation. Mary Kate looked down demurely and said, "Thank you, but my Spanish is so much better than my French." She and Ruth, her Spanish teacher, then treated us to a duet of "Feliz Navidad."

Speech and language do not come easily for persons with Down's syndrome and represent one of their greatest sources of frustration. It takes courage for many who are retarded to risk being understood in their native tongue, let alone a foreign language. Love like Ruth's uses imagination to fuel courage.

The most gripping description of the prophetic role of the Down's syndrome individual is in Morris West's novel, *Clowns of God*. West's vision of Jesus' second coming describes the returned Christ with a Down's child on his knee, serving her eucharistic bread and wine.

> What better [sign] could I give than to make this little one whole and new? I could do it; but I will not. . . . I gave this mite a gift I denied to all of you—eternal innocence. . . . She will never offend me, as all of you have done. She will never pervert or destroy the works of my Father's hands. She is necessary to you. She will evoke the kindness that will keep you human. . . . She will remind you every day that I AM WHO I AM.[20]

Since the overall life expectancy for children with cancer has improved and the life-opportunities for people with Down's syndrome have advanced, more of God's prophetic clowns are with us. Each time I partake of the bread and wine, I am reminded of their kindness and the many ways they keep me human.

6

Invitation to a Feast

*May our lives be a feast: the spirit of
Jesus in our midst, the work of Jesus
in our hands, the spirit of Jesus in
our work.*

J. Metternich Team, "Unser Leben"[21]

Recently I breakfasted at a medium-grade diner where I heard a man warn his son in rapid-fire Spanish that if the kid didn't stop whining and eat his bagel, he wouldn't get to go to McDonald's for lunch. The father had unleashed the penultimate parental weapon and by golly, it worked. Each of us has our own concept of an ideal feast. The feast I long for most, however, has nothing to do with cholesterol-burdened beef and fries. Because of my acquaintance with children with cancer, I am probably bidden to more soul-fortifying repasts than most have the opportunity to attend. May I invite you to a feast?

At the climax to the story of the healing of Simon Peter's mother-in-law is a feast: "Now Simon's mother-in-law was suffering from a high fever, and they asked [Jesus] about her. Then he stood over her and rebuked the fever, and it left her. Immediately she got up and began to serve them" (Luke 4:38–39, NRSV). She rises from her sickbed and serves a meal to Jesus and the disciples. The story is so important that it is included by three of the four gospel writers.

I cannot read this Bible story without thinking of Donny, my little Down's syndrome saint who taught me a great deal about the joy of servanthood. Part of his treatment included administering morphine, which moved silently and painlessly through a small butterfly needle taped to the skin of his abdomen. Donny called the device his "beeper" and smothered it with Smurf stickers. He was Doctor Donny, on call. For this nine-year-old "doctor" with Down's syndrome, the small battery-operated pump anchored to his pajama waist made it possible for him to stay at home and control the pain that accompanies terminal leukemia.

Hospice nurses came to adjust the dosage from time to time, and Donny moved from his bedroom to the living room where Smurf-bedecked sheets and pillowcases transformed the couch into a most acceptable base of operations. He had more friends than most of us will have in longer lifetimes and could visit with them in between snoozes. As the leukemia progressed, he had less energy and more cat naps. My phone rang one evening after the nurse had visited Donny's home and told his parents that he might die that very night. His mother called to ask my opinion.

When I arrived, Donny was dozing peacefully on his Smurf sofa, surrounded by a half-dozen assorted friends. He was paler than when I had last seen him, but his pulse was steady. "I went out of the prophecy business a long time ago," I told them. "I wish I could be sure, but you know how unpredictable these things are."

As if on cue, Donny rose from his "deathbed" with a luxuriant yawn. The Prince of Smurfs was hungry and decided to take his guests "out" to dinner. He assumed the role of *maitre d'hôtel* at a mythical restaurant and escorted us to our tables.

Invisible pad and pen poised in his hand, Donny went from guest to guest, reciting the specials of the evening. For each guest, a different ethnic restaurant was presented with a complete selection from *suppe* to *nuez*. After he took the order from his last guest (in a Mexican restaurant), he flopped back into Smurfland and resumed his nap with a self-satisfied sigh of contentment.

"It won't be tonight," I confidently prophesied, and Donny grinned in his sleep. A month later, he died. For years afterward, Ruth continued to find Smurfs in closets and drawers where he hid them for her to find.

To some, the gospel story of Simon Peter's mother-in-law reads as if she was healed just in time to do slave duty for the men-folk. In countless ways, my patients have been my servants and it is an irony for me that I find myself called to follow in their footsteps in an era when some women feel called to move "beyond servanthood."[22] It is precisely because Jesus, the Master of paradox, does *not* call me servant, but rather friend, that I know myself as his servant *as well as* his friend.

Tony and I first met when he was nine years old, and because of his illness, we were an important part of each other's lives for seven years. His life was drawing to a close as I prepared for a sabbatical year away from Yale. His parents knew that I would probably be out of the country when he died, but we protected each other from telling Tony. The colleague who would care for him in my absence gently chided me for my cowardice.

His mom worried that I didn't know how deeply Tony felt about me, although I never really felt uninformed. He had written letters to all his brothers, but he never thought to say good-bye to me. We both always assumed that we would be together for his departure from this life.

I received an invitation to his home for a dinner that he himself would prepare. On his next clinic visit, Tony reviewed the menu with me, watching my eyes carefully for a hint of the respect due a chef of such competence. En route to his home for that meal, my beeper indicated an emergency page. The chef had been taken to a nearby hospital with uncontrollable seizures. The dinner was postponed. Tony was never quite the same after that episode. Intellectually and physically he was diminished, but spiritually he was stronger.

We eventually did share a dinner of quiche and other of Tony's favorites at his home. After dinner, he invited me to his holy of holies to see his baseball card collection and plot my biorhythms on his computer. Several weeks later, the same computer drafted me a letter. He was afraid that I did not know how he felt about me and shared his love and his mischief in a letter that revealed all the nicknames he had for me and my colleagues. I'm glad to know he considered me "Kompetent."

My colleagues wrote to me in Germany to tell me how Tony outlived all medical expectations. At Christmas, I flew home and had the opportunity for a visit with my young friend. He was hospitalized in order to receive a new medication but was in good health and spirits. We faced off, bed to bedside, sizing each other up. I noticed that his hair had regrown and his face was no longer bloated from prednisone. He read my thoughts and countered, "Your hair is grayer but you've lost weight. Do you dare to eat a quiche?"

Towards the end of our Christmas visit, both Tony and I ran out of words and nodded in farewell. As I walked out of the room to return to Germany, he said softly, "Auf wiederseh'n." It would turn out that I was not there when eastertide became his Easter time.

Lord, now let thy servant (thy served) depart in peace, according to thy word.

7

Learning a New Language

*If I speak in the tongues of mortals
and of angels, but do not have love,
I am a noisy gong or a clanging
cymbal.*

1 Corinthians 13:1 (NRSV)

*L*anguage can be a vehicle for communication and comfort, or, like in the case of the Tower of Babel, it can result in confusion and alienation. Words have tremendous power over us. For some of us, learning a new way to speak (and listen) is a requirement before we can achieve the untroubled heart that Jesus promised.

In our fearful society, *cancer* is possibly the most dreaded of words. During a recent hospitalization for minor surgery, I recuperated postoperatively on the gynecological oncology floor. My disease was neither gynecological nor malignant but this was the only floor of our hospital that had a bed available.

Some of my friends were so disturbed to find me on a cancer ward that my nurses worried that I, too, might be upset with my room assignment. A psychotherapist I know was highly agitated by the idea: "I know you keep saying that there are worse things in life than cancer, but I sure have a hard time thinking of any. I had the same surgery a few years ago, and if I had woken up on that ward, it would have upset me a lot."

Is it possible to talk the language of cancer and have freedom from fear? Intellectual knowledge about cancer does not seem to protect us against this primordial dread.

Fear is something with which we as humans are very familiar. The Bible says that fear is so typical a human response that visiting angels were careful to preface their remarks with "Be not afraid," even when they came bearing good news.

Although I may not have a heightened fear of cancer, I do know about the emotion of fear. Several years ago I had to take a medication with a peculiar side effect. I would start talking and find the thought suspended in mid-air, incomplete. I would literally have to wait for the thought to take a different path or for the lazy synapse in my brain to finally fire. It was a devastating experience, since I could not do my work if I did not have quick access to words. Lives depend on my quick-firing brain. Never in my life have I been more depressed or more afraid.

I remember praying at the time, "Lord, take my life but don't touch one neuron of my beautiful brain." As soon as the prayer was prayed, I realized its folly. It was painful to realize that my adult relationship with God was grounded in intellectual apprehension and a half-brained spirituality. I may give lip service to the spiritual gifts of the retarded, but was I really ready to be equal with someone like Donny?

I was not the only one whose life was influenced by Donny. Roger's personal struggle with cancer was a particularly difficult one. A teenager, he endured chemotherapy impatiently and with great anguish. When the first program failed to cure him, he faced more rigorous treatment. But he was unwilling to talk about it and unable to find meaning in his own predicament.

Roger's friends had trouble in their attempts at helping him, until one high-school classmate invited Roger to training sessions for the Special Olympics at the local center for the retarded and handicapped. There Roger met Donny and was caught up by the infectious love of the Down's syndrome children who reached out and touched him. He volunteered to accompany them to the state Special Olympics.

Roger approached his treatment the next week quite differently. With chemotherapy running in a vein but showing a radiant face, he asked me, "Do you know I went to the Special Olympics and met Donny? It changed my life!"

❧   ❧   ❧

Some of us are quick with our tongues and yet others find their tongues a natural hindrance. Artie was Tom's brother. Tom, you will remember, died in his bedroom shortly after he had a vision of Jesus visiting him in a garden. Tom had shared the dream with his Down's syndrome brother, Artie. The morning of Tom's death, Artie had nothing to say, but he packed his books and went to the curb to wait for the school bus as he always did. His parents wondered how, in his simplicity, he had processed that loss. It was as though nothing unusual had happened in his life that day.

In the months that followed Tom's death, Artie was consumed with his own activities, preparing for the winter competition of the Special Olympics. Artie's performance was truly amazing, the ski champion's neck bowing under the many medals. Bursting with pride, he joined the other athletes for a press conference.

"This has been a very exciting day, Artie," said the sportscaster. "What were you thinking about when you crossed the finish line?"

Ordinarily, Artie's speech is very difficult to understand, but his response was clearly heard: "My brother died this year."

"I'm sure he was an inspiration to you," replied the stunned sportscaster.

"Yes!" answered Artie.

Wolf Wolfensberger calls this phenomenon "speaking in tongues"—a person whose ordinary speech is unintelligible suddenly speaks clearly, revealing an important truth.[23] Sometimes, modern technology helps in the interpretation of those tongues. Linguists in California find that some Down's syndrome children with faulty speech are freed to express themselves quite poetically by the keyboard of a computer. A teenager named Christine chose to write about God and turned to the researcher to say, "He's gonna like this." I am sure she is right. She wrote, "I like God's finest whispers."[24]

A children's hospital is a school for fine whispers where most of the students are parents. A mother in Wisconsin whose eight-year-old daughter died twenty-five years ago wrote to tell me what she learned:

> Many times we said that we thought she was a little missionary sent from God. We, her family, have been taught so much through her. Becky told us that she had the most wonderful prayer in her heart to God. A little later she said, "Do you know what God said to me in my heart? He said, 'Yea, though ye walk through the valley of the shadow of death, ye shall fear no evil.'" Then she added, "Nothing could break the chain from my heart to God's heart—nothing in the world."[25]

Donny's family teaches me that the origin of prayer is in the soul, not in the head. During a hospitalization for a blood-borne infection, his parents lamented his terminal condition and their lack of preparedness for his death. "We don't want him to suffer, but we are not ready for him to die. We pray that God will not take him yet."

Several days later, he was discharged without further treatment. Without antibiotics, his fever resolved; and without chemotherapy, his leukemic cells were replaced by normal white blood cells capable of fighting infection. This "spontaneous" remission lasted long enough for him to die at home many months later surrounded by family and his many friends.

Before the diagnosis of cancer, many of my patients and their parents do not have much experience in listening for these whispers. Tony and his family attended church regularly, but prayer became a new language for him when his leukemia advanced to his brain as well as his bone marrow. It was time to prepare his family for the inevitable and, along with the medical details of clinical death, I mentioned the religious experiences that other families have described.

He recovered from this particular episode, but some weeks later, his mother reported that, out of the blue, Tony said, "He wants me."

His mother was frightened but found the courage to ask, "Do you mean God?"

When he answered in the affirmative, his mother asked him if God spoke to him in a dream.

"No. He speaks to me when I pray."

"What do you mean, when you pray?"

"I start praying and then I listen."

"Is it scary?"

"No. It's peaceful."

A frightened mother chose just to listen. Some weeks later, he said, "I don't want to die yet. Gerry is only three and is not old enough to understand. I've been able to talk to each of my other brothers to prepare them and they'll be okay. I can leave a letter for Gerry, but it's not the same. If I could live just one more year, I could explain it to him myself and he will understand. Three is just too young."

I explained to the mother that it was just not medically possible for him to survive that additional year. Tony lived for exactly one year after that honorable prayer.

❧ ❧ ❧

Sometimes a new language is learned through dreams. One of my patients was a three-month-old baby boy who was admitted to the hospital with a cancer that had begun in the adrenal gland and had now spread to the liver. I had few encouraging words as I made rounds. My heart went out to Naomi, the young mother who sat at her firstborn's cribside.

"Do you believe in healing?" she asked. She and her husband were raised in a mainline Protestant church and had not returned since their wedding. Their early married life was full and happy, but their baby's desperate situation now made her ask whether something important was missing.

Naomi knew a woman whose life was changed by a charismatic renewal experience. This woman often retreated into a room in her home that she had converted into a shrine for healing prayer. At the same time she grew increasingly alienated from her husband, who did not share these beliefs and practices. In her time of crisis, Naomi wanted to seek all possible alternatives that might help her child, but she was frightened that such a search might damage her marriage as it had her friend's.

I shared with Naomi some of the struggles that others have faced with that question. I told her that I hoped that if she prayed for her son, Henry, to be healed, she would also be willing to ask her husband to join her to put their lives in God's hands, whether or not Henry lived.

That weekend, she and Jim, her husband, asked a hospital chaplain to baptize the baby and pray for his healing. On Monday, Henry was a little better, but Naomi's appearance was transformed. She told me of the events of the weekend and said, "I don't know if Henry will be healed, but I feel as if I've been healed."

When the baby did not survive, I wondered how one could "find God" while hoping for healing or how one could stay faithful after that hope had vanished. Several years later, Naomi wrote to me to tell me of a dream she had. She dreamed that she and the baby were in the kitchen of the church where she grew up. Henry was crawling around on the floor, and every time he got to a certain place in the center, he'd say, "God!" He was very happy, like a child greeting a well-known and trusted friend—or parent.

In her dream, Naomi commented to a friend, who was also in the church kitchen, that it gave her goose-bumps. It was as though Henry could see God, although she and her friend could not. Then, the next time he reached the center, Henry died. His legs buckled under him, and he threw his head back to look at her once more and reached out an arm. Naomi rushed over to him and grabbed his hand, but it was too late. His eyes were blank and he was dead.

"Suddenly, God strode in and scooped up my little one and perched him upon his arm. Henry sat on God's arm with a hand on God's shoulder, laughing and chattering with him." Naomi could see that the baby was fine and happy and that he knew God well, but she was sad that she could not hold him anymore. "God saw how sad I was and felt sorry for me, and so he handed Henry to me and said I could keep him for a while longer until he returned from the mission he had to go on. Henry was fine now, although not as animated with me, and I held him. It was as though he had been handed from a Parent to a trusted babysitter." He was in her arms, but watching God.

As God was leaving, Naomi asked, "Will I have other children I can keep?" She goes on, "God stopped and looked at me with so much love, it was overwhelming. He said gently, in a way that made me feel especially cared for, 'Everyone's life has a plan.'" Naomi held Henry's cheek to her own and tried to figure out whether God's look had betrayed any sorrow (that she would not get her wish) or amusement (that good things were ahead for her). "But there was neither, just love, overwhelming love. That was what mattered and that was what the answer was—not yes or no, but God's love."

In the years since the baby's death, Naomi and Jim became the proud parents of two healthy babies. Perhaps it's an occupational hazard, but since this mysterious dream-prayer was shared, I have tried many times to *analyze* it. While my attempts at understanding the dream have always fallen short, I have found that each time I have *told* her story, someone says that they, like Naomi, were "healed."

One of the Greek words in the New Testament for healing implies salvation. Spiritual healing does not restore a person to the place they were before the illness. It provides a more comprehensive health care package. The peace and healing of God that defies human understanding can bring us salvation and keep our hearts and minds untroubled—even when they do not satisfy our analytical inclinations!

8

Angels and Other Strangers

Do not neglect to show hospitality to strangers, for by doing that some have entertained angels without knowing it.

Hebrews 13:2 (NRSV)

*S*keptics who attempt to minimize the importance of near-death experiences of adults claim that these phenomena are culturally determined. Similar comments have been used to write off the spiritual utterances of precocious children with cancer.

I had a phone call from a reporter who was following up on a wire-service report of my work with terminally ill children. "Did any of the children say what Jesus looked like?" he asked.

I am not sure what he thought of my response: "You know, the children weren't exactly sitting there with pen and pad poised to take notes in case they later ran into a skeptical adult. The only story I can tell you is what he *doesn't* look like."

I once heard a story of a young child who was not ill, but died unexpectedly in an accident. On an occasion prior to her death, she looked up at an artist's rendition of Jesus and said emphatically, "He doesn't look like that at all!" This child's story is not unique. It manifests one of the most remarkable qualities of children.

༒ ༒ ༒

When Ann married, she gave up her nominal Christian belief since it seemed irrelevant to her new life. Although she and her husband were economically privileged, romance faded early and she soon considered her marriage a disaster. But the lifestyle, including a new mink coat, had its rewards, and she adored her youngest son, T. J. She told a friend, once, that if anything happened to this marvelous five-year-old, they would have to lock her up.

Ann had never sent the children to Sunday school, and the name of God was never mentioned in their house. One day, T. J. said out of the blue, "Mama, I love you more than *anything* in the world, except God. And I love him a little bit more!"

She was taken aback and told him that this was okay as long as it was God he loved more than her. "But why would he speak of God?" she pondered. Even more mysterious was why he should love a God whose name he had never heard from her lips.

Two days later was one of the coldest days of a bitterly cold winter. While his sister was horseback riding, T. J. crossed a snow-covered creek and broke through the ice. He must have died immediately, although it took the family an hour and a half to find him. The first words out of Ann's mouth when she heard the news was, "I hate you, God!"

But even as she spit out the words, she felt herself held in loving arms. Can you truly hate someone whom you have never in some way loved?

As her world shattered around her, she remembered another mysterious thing that T. J. did that week. He had bought a Christmas gift for her at the Secret Santa shop at school and kept trying to give it to her before Christmas. Each time he tried to give it to her, she laughed and told him to put it away until Christmas. He was persistent but she prevailed. When she got home from the stables where he died, she ran upstairs to the place he kept it and opened it. Inside she found a beautiful necklace with a cross.

As Ann looks back now, she says that Jesus dealt with her the way a loving parent deals with a hurt child. "He made me reach out to others rather than get lost in myself. Helping others helped me." Prior to the accident, Ann's husband had no religious belief, but he cried out to God for help and sensed an immediate response to his prayer. Slowly, their old materialistic lives melted away, their marriage healed, and they described themselves as new creatures in Christ.

Through her ordeal, Ann discovered she had a gift of spiritual hospitality, bringing healing to other parents. Henri Nouwen characterizes healing as a form of hospitality:

> Healing means, first of all, the creation of an empty but friendly space where those who suffer can tell their story to someone who can listen with real attention.

Healers are hosts who patiently and carefully listen to the story of the suffering stranger. Patients are guests who rediscover their selves by telling their story to the one who offers them a place to stay.[26]

This young mother has reached out to over 200 families whose children suffered accidental deaths. In sharing her own story, Ann has learned that many parents felt that their children knew they were going to die. She calls her effort "T. J. Ministries," not only after her T. J., but to emphasize how she has made it since then—*T*hrough *J*esus.

❧ ❧ ❧

Not all strangers are unknown to each other. Some become strangers to each other through the painful process of failed marriage and divorce. This represents one of the most difficult situations in my practice. There is an enormous additional burden when family strife accompanies the seriously ill child to the hospital. Because of divorce and remarriage, my young patient Bill had four parents. Bill's prayer was for them to be one family, with one heart and a new spirit.

At the time he was diagnosed with leukemia, Bill's biological parents and stepparents thought they were doing their best to survive divorce, remarriage, and the sharing of children. What helped them most was living far away from each other and limiting their social intercourse to small-talk at drop-off and pick-up exchanges of the children. They were more successful than most families in similar situations and Bill certainly did not seem damaged by belonging to a less-than-old-fashioned American family unit. In fact, it was in the context of the reorganized family that he began to think about God.

The initial contact of the quartet of parents in the hospital was highly civil. When the stress of former spouses in daily contact finally hit, this group did the unprecedented. They knew the root source of their stress and rather than displacing their family anger onto the medical staff, they talked to each other. Kathy was shocked to realize that she had more in common with her ex-husband's new wife than any other woman in her acquaintance. The mother and stepmother formed a nucleus for reconciliation and communication.

When Bill relapsed and his death appeared inevitable, he indicated a desire to die at home. In attempting to honor that request, we found that it would not be medically easy. He came to our hospital from a distant region that had no type of hospice care. With the help of a nurse in that community who volunteered to make home visits, the four parents lived under the same roof, sharing the nursing responsibilities. After Bill died, they invited me to dinner.

The two mothers worked together in the kitchen on the meal. The house was in need of repairs, though during the last weeks of Bill's illness, the two fathers had made significant progress. They had shopped together to buy me a gift and spoke of their future plans.

They talked about the holidays to come. No other friends or family members could really understand the anticipated emptiness of the year to come. Bill's birthday was near Christmas, and the holidays for all of them had become irrevocably tied to that event. They planned to spend all the holidays, from Thanksgiving through the New Year, as an extended family. Through Bill and in Christ, they had been reconciled.

≈ ≈ ≈

In human terms, the battle lines of truth and evil seem never more easily drawn than in a failing marriage and divorce. In each such personal "holy war" for truth, the enemy seems only too clear to envision. Yet Christian philosopher Richard Mouw warns us that

> The only two actors in the cosmic drama whose performances [for good and evil] we can count on are God and Satan. Once we get to the level of human performance, the lines are more difficult to draw. . . . We will often misidentify truths and errors if we think in rigid "us versus them" categories. We would do well to exercise caution in how we draw the battle lines.[27]

Child psychiatrist Albert Solnit knows that he is not using paradigms of the judicial system when he suggests that divorced parents should apply the wisdom of Solomon and the Golden Rule rather than to look out for their own interests in child custody.[28] Solnit points out that the court too often looks to the interests of the adults and wields the knife over the child to satisfy the parents, even when it would fatally divide the child.

Philosopher Mouw's and psychiatrist Solnit's words are wise, albeit seemingly impossible in terms of human understanding. And yet, we are promised that the wolf shall dwell with the lamb. The prophet Isaiah also says that in that day of the humanly impossible, a little child shall lead them.

9

Does Jesus Drive a School Bus?

*Children have to be educated but
they also have to be left to educate
themselves.*

Ernest Dimnet, *The Art of Thinking*

A colleague told me of an eight-year-old boy with cancer whose parents avoided discussing death or matters of faith despite obvious signs that their son would die within a few days. The boy took them by surprise one morning with the report of a dream. A big yellow school bus pulled up to his house in the dream and the door opened. On the bus he saw Jesus, who told him of his impending death and invited him to go with him on the bus. In his dream, he accepted Jesus' invitation. It was with great peace that he recounted this dream to his parents.

Of all of the images children have come up with, the school bus has become my favorite. So I was puzzled when I told this story to child psychiatrist Kyle Pruett and watched his brow furrow solemnly. Was there a psychoanalytical interpretation at variance with the Christian message I read into the dream? He narrated the significance of the school bus from a loving father's point of view.[29]

Several weeks before our conversation, the entire Pruett family drove the eldest daughter to begin her college career in a distant state. As they neared their destination, Kyle was confronted by a memory from his daughter's childhood that returned to him unbidden. "We were at the curb on her first day of kindergarten and I could see that big, old yellow school bus pull up. I could even see, hear, and feel that huge door *slam* in my face, taking my daughter away from me. I had completely forgotten how wrenching an experience that was for me—not at all nice!"

At a nursery school where Dr. Pruett consults, the model of a yellow school bus is worn out and requires replacement faster than any other toy. In playing with the bus, these youngsters master separation from their parents. If children must master separation from their parents, the converse must also be true: parents must master separation from their children. But this presupposes an earlier step. Ethicist William May reminds us that the first task of parenthood is to master *attachment* to the "little stranger."[30]

May warns us that the baby's arrival upsets the myth that a child will extend the familiar. Instead, it pushes the parents into the novel and strange. On the wards of my own hospital, we mourn the fact that in our own modern world, not enough parents master attachment to their children. In the same medical center where we miraculously rejuvenate lungs, livers, and bone marrows, we cannot seem to save children sickened by social despair.

A colleague, who works in behavioral pediatrics, commented to me, "The children's psychiatric ward is really getting me down. Isn't it ironic that I come to talk to you, an *oncologist*, to cheer up? Tell me some of your stories about your patients. I want to feel good. What kind of crazy world is this?"

Part of the craziness in the world are the rules that some physicians make to distance themselves from patients. A colleague hesitated to write to a family when their daughter came to mind a year after her death. He was concerned that contact from the medical staff would make the family sad and invade their privacy. He shared this concern some time later at an informal meeting of our staff with the child's father. "What's the worst thing that could happen to me?" smiled this big ex-football player. "I might cry? Big deal!"

A young physician commented that he had read in a textbook that it was pathological for grieving to extend more than a year after the death. The dad's eyes gleamed moistly, "Do you really think that a day goes by that I *don't* think about her? That doesn't mean that life doesn't go on or I am unable to function. How could I *ever* forget her?"

Another father whose professional field is communication used his computer to compose dialogue with his son about daily family life and how he feels in the years following the young man's death. A mother whose child died seven years ago cannot trim a Christmas tree without thinking of her son standing by her side, backseat driving the placement of each ornament. "Can a mother forget her child?" analogizes the God who promises never to forget us.

❧ ❧ ❧

I recently met a young couple who lost identical twins to the same disease. Nathan and Jordan loved school buses and would ask every visitor to their home to draw a school bus with Jesus, their parents and grandparents, and them aboard. Nate was never able to walk and died at three years of age, three months before his brother, Jordan.

Shortly before Nate's death, the entire family went on a trip on a school bus that turned out to be a disaster. The driver went too fast over a pothole and they were all roughly thrown around. Little Nate was thrown into the aisle and his mom caught him just in time to prevent serious injury. This upset the twins very much and made it very important for them to know who drove a school bus. Dr. Pruett recalls the same preoccupation of his daughters. At the dinner table, the family would often hear the comparative merits (and demerits) of the current driver. It mattered very much who was in control of that school bus.

Although they knew that they would lose the second little guy, these young parents bravely attempted to answer Jordan's questions about death, heaven, and his brother. They were never able to begin the process of grieving for Nathan as long as they faced the unfinished business of Jordan's impending death. Remembering the rough ride in the bus, Jordan commented, "Nate with Jesus. Nate no more owies."

A few days after Nathan's funeral, Jordan asked his aunt, "What Nate doing?" Auntie stretched her imagination to paint a picture for him: "Well, I bet Nate's running in the grass with Jesus with no shoes on!" "Silly Nate!" exclaimed the little one as he laughed and gazed upward, as if to see his brother, who could not even walk in his lifetime, running with Jesus.

This became his favorite image of heaven, and when he went for a walk he would insist on walking through the tall grass at the side of the road. A month later, he told his grandmother, "Oma, Nate's running through the grass with Jesus. Nate no shoes on. Nate all better."

The parents choked back their tears each time Jordan would ask to go pick Nathan up to bring him home. Whenever he asked to go to see his brother in heaven, he accepted their answer of, "Soon, Jordan, you will go to see Jesus and Nathan in heaven."

One day he became very thoughtful for a moment, thinking of his brother and how he would get to heaven to join him. He asked, "Dad, does Jesus drive a school bus?"

10

Surviving the Holocaust

Has all this suffering, this dying around us, a meaning? For, if not, then ultimately there is no meaning to survival; for a life whose meaning depends upon such a happenstance—as whether one escapes or not—ultimately would not be worth living at all.

Viktor Frankl, *Man's Search for Meaning*

I would like to end this book with the previous chapter, to simply witness that God is alive, interested, and loving. I would like to say amen with the children safe in the arms of Jesus.

But I was recently reminded by a parent that belief can be a more painful proposition than unbelief. The unbeliever assumes that no One is responsible or holds an answer. Belief to these parents suggests that there is some One who holds all answers. For every young heart untroubled, there may be one or more older hearts left thirsty and unsure.

A year before Tony died, I had to give him a spinal treatment. My beloved young friend choked back his tears as he entered the treatment room although we both knew he would cooperate. The dirty deed would be done with no discussion, without a struggle. I had feelings of anger and frustration that day and my feelings poured upward: "Don't you care at all?"

I personally hold that there is no pain on this earth to compare with the loss of a child. If there is such a thing as the survival of the fittest, the fit surely do not seem very fit to accept their survival. For every holocaust, there is a variation on the "survivors' syndrome."

ε&ε&ε&

When I was a medical student, I participated in the interview of a patient admitted to a psychiatric hospital for depression. The patient was a Jew who survived Hitler's "final solution." His young daughter did not survive, however, and he could not forget the day that her fate was decided. The inmates were paraded before a guard to decide who would be chosen for slave labor and who would be used for "medical experimentation." This man walked hand in hand with his daughter as they approached the guard.

The guard indicated that the father should join the labor force to the left but his daughter, the group to the right. As they understood the implication, his daughter held his hand tighter and begged her papa to protect her. The impatient soldier poised his bayonet over their clutched hands in unambiguous threat. As the child grasped her father's hand the tighter, the guard suddenly lowered the bayonet and this poor man let go of his daughter's hand. She was led away to the right and to her death. He survived but was haunted for the rest of his life by the fact that he had let go of her hand. He saw her death as his own fault.

There are countless ways a parent can perceive that he or she has let go of the child's hand. A mother whose son was three years old when he developed cancer called a few years ago to tell me a story and ask me a question. Arthur, her son, had multiple relapses and was close to death many times, but he did survive and his potential mortality from cancer was no longer an issue.

What she wished to share were the circumstances surrounding this child's conception. If there was a way for her to turn back the clock, she never would have attempted to abort her pregnancy. She was not married to the child's father and he did not want this child. He offered her a medication that he was assured would terminate her pregnancy. When the pregnancy was not aborted, he threw her out.

Her question to me many years later was, "Do you think that the concoction I drank caused the cancer?"

I told her that we will never know what caused the cancer, but that it was not possible to live so many years keeping that memory to herself without suffering from the burden. She later wrote that although her own religious tradition preached forgiveness through acceptance of Christ's sacrifice, she had never been able to forgive herself and had rejected the forgiveness that God offered in Jesus.

She felt there was no one in her church with whom she could share this burden. Everyone would have been shocked that she had been so sinful. Others might have advised her that sin is a projection of too powerful a superego. After "confessing" to me, she underlined every passage in her Bible that referred to

God's forgiveness. She was amazed that the burden was finally lifted. She had finally forgiven herself. The healing of memories can be more difficult to accomplish than the healing of cancer. Her son, Arthur, has been in remission and presumably cured for more than a couple of decades.

I have watched over the years to observe, not which Scripture passages are recommended to these parents by their pastors, but what parts of the Bible they seek on their own. There are three passages that they study and restudy: Jesus in the Garden of Gethsemane, the story of Job, and the story of Abraham and Isaac on Mount Moriah. Death-camp survivor and historian Elie Wiesel reminds us that Abraham was asked on the mount literally to bring the only son he loved and to bind him to the altar for a holocaust.

It is my observation that parents tend to see their child's illness most often in terms of their own failure. In fact, when I am asked, "Do you know why children get cancer?" I always assume the real question is, "What did *I* do wrong that *my* child got cancer?"

Wiesel tells us that one unusual Midrashic (Jewish commentary on the Scripture) explanation of the *Akeda* (Hebrew name for the story of Mount Moriah) attributes God's challenge to Abraham as punishment for his rejection of his other son, Ishmael.[31]

What was father Abraham thinking on the way up the mount? Where did he find the courage to take the first step toward what was promised to be a horrible death of his beloved son and his own dreams? Psychiatrist and Holocaust survivor Viktor Frankl tells of an old Viennese saying that he used in counseling fearful patients: It is better to have a horrible ending than to experience horror without ending.[32] Faith would rather take the first step toward what would seem to be a holocaust than live through a thousand imaginary holocausts without end. Father Abraham was put to a test of faith in the face of a holocaust and so was son Viktor.

ع‌ ع‌ ع‌

As the Nazi nightmare continued to ravage Austria and countless Jews were deported from Vienna, Viktor Frankl waited for his visa to emigrate to the United States before it was too late. He feared, however, what would happen to his elderly parents if he were to leave. The day the coveted visa arrived, the burden of his parents' potential fate lay heavily on his heart. He covered the yellow *Judenstern* on his jacket lapel with his briefcase and entered Stephansdom, Vienna's main cathedral, in time for the Wednesday concert. As the organist played, Frankl wrestled in his soul.

He arrived home to find his father excited about a piece of marble that he held in his hands. On his walk that day, his father passed by the destroyed synagogue and found this broken piece. It was a part of the sacred law, a fragment of eternal truth rescued from the hideous rubble of National Socialism. Father and son looked together to see which of the commandments it represented. The single Hebrew letter gave the clue: "Honor thy father and thy mother that thy days may be long upon the land."[33]

In the Old Testament, father Abraham had the outrageous faith to believe that God would honor his promise to make Abraham the father of many nations. In another era, son Viktor had the outrageous faith to give up his visa to certain freedom and remain in the Nazi-occupied land with his vulnerable parents. He was able to protect them for several more years and went with them to the camps where both his mother and father met their deaths. Frankl survived to tell his patients and the world about self-sacrificing love. God's law and its promises were written on his heart.

My own Mount Moriah looms on the horizon.

11

Facing Mount Moriah

Abraham took the wood of the burnt offering and laid it on his son Isaac and he himself carried the fire and the knife. So the two of them walked on together.

Genesis 22:6 (NRSV)

*A*braham hears a voice say, "I am the Lord, thy God. Thou shalt have no other gods before me."

"By all means, Lord," he replies with pious courtesy. "The new BMW, a fancier house, a summer cottage on the beach—they mean nothing to me anymore. I've learned my lesson. I denounce keeping up with the Joneses."

"Abraham!" comes the voice, now louder. "Thou shalt have no other gods before me!"

"I heard you, Lord. Believe me I have denounced my workaholic ways. Nothing is more important to me than my family. I denounce any worldly ambitions that would separate me from my family. I place power, ambition, riches, fame all on the altar. You have gotten your point across. Trust me."

"Abraham, Abraham! Thou shalt have no other gods before me!"

❧ ❧ ❧

Many of the parents I meet start their journeys thinking that this is the answer. They used to live shallow, materialistic lives, and they now hear God saying that there is something better for them. For many fathers, work has alienated them from their wives and children, and so they naturally assume that God's message is simply to invest more time in their families. Certainly this is a healthy part of the message, but few suspect that it is not the whole story.

↝ ↝ ↝

"For God's sake, I'm getting a headache!" complains Abraham. "What other gods could you possibly mean? I've covered a lot of territory in my time and heard about a lot of so-called gods but none of those pathetic idols can compare to you, Yahweh! Besides, you and I have a covenant."

"Ah, the covenant, Abraham. Do you love me more than the covenant?"

"What are you talking about, Yahweh? Of course I do. A covenant is a concept. You are the Living God."

"The covenant is through your seed Isaac. Abraham, do you love me more than Isaac?"

Abraham turns pale. Isaac senses his dis-ease and grasps his papa's hand tightly.

↝ ↝ ↝

Jesus restated it this way: "Whoever comes to me and does not hate father and mother, wife and children, brothers and sisters, yes, and even life itself, cannot be my disciple" (Luke 14:26, NRSV).

ঽ ঽ ঽ

"Hate my child?" thunders Abraham. "What are you talking about, God? Have you forgotten what Isaac was all about? He's the seed for the covenant. Without my child, you have no covenant, no people, no future on this meshuginah planet.

"You're changing the rules, Yahweh," he continues. "Have you heard the joke going around the Jewish community since the Holocaust, Yahweh? 'Chosen people, huh? Next time, choose somebody else.'"

"Abraham, Abraham, Abraham! Thou shalt have no other gods before me!"

ঽ ঽ ঽ

For those of us who have not given life to another human being, our lives may still bear fruit that is at risk of becoming an idol. I ask myself who or what my own Isaac is, as I sit at the word processor at two in the morning lovingly shaping and rewriting this manuscript.

"Di, do you hate the book for my sake?"

"What are you talking about, Lord? Isn't the book your work?"

"Which do you love more, Di, the God of Abraham, Isaac, and Jacob or your book about the God of Abraham, Isaac, and Jacob?"

The problem with holocausts is that we learn that even the professed believer may worship a graven image that barely resembles the Creator, Redeemer, and Sustainer of the universe. Viktor Frankl went to Auschwitz with the pages of a manuscript secreted in his coat, only to be forced to part with his coat once he arrived. He describes his grieving for the loss of that work: "Thus I had to undergo and to overcome the loss of my mental child. And now it seemed as if nothing and no one would survive me; neither a physical or mental child of my own!"[34]

Instead of his own coat with the hidden book, he inherited the tattered rags of someone who was sent directly to the gas chamber on arrival. Coincidence is not a term that he would choose to accept for what he discovered in the pocket of this garment: "Instead of the many pages of my manuscript, I found in a pocket of the newly acquired coat one single page torn out of a Hebrew prayer book, containing the most important Jewish prayer, *Shema Yisrael.*" (Found in Deuteronomy 6:4–5, the prayer reads, "Hear, O Israel: The LORD is our God, the LORD alone. You shall love the LORD your God with all your heart, and with all your soul, and with all your might" [NRSV].)

A colleague came to my office, troubled about the mother of one of his patients. "She's lost her faith," he worries. "She prayed that the child would be healed. Now she is angry at God."

A nurse expressed concern about a father who sits in his son's room rereading the same passages of the Bible that he had claimed in faith that his son would be healed. Now he is frightened and angry, but he keeps reading all the same.

These parents may be angry enough to "hate" God, but they have not lost their belief. True atheists should be at peace with thwarted prayers, not restlessly angry at the Nonexistent and everyone who does believe. They have not lost the true God but simply come to the brokenness of the truly spiritual person who must resign from trying to be God for their loved ones. During the dark night of the soul, they are angry at the world's most patient Lover.

ॐ ॐ ॐ

As helpful as our own families may be, as constrained as we may be to honor them, on Mount Moriah we are like orphaned children, on our own. It is on Moriah that we learn that our parents, our traditions, our culture have added jots and tittles to the law. The first commandment remains simple, to have no other gods before God. Our task on Moriah is to learn what this means in our own families, in our own times, and in our own traditions. On Moriah we are alone with God.

Old Testament theologian Phyllis Trible believes Abraham's faith was challenged because of his idolatry of his son. Abraham had allowed Isaac to replace Yah-weh as the primary object of his adoration. She sees the resolution of Abraham's test as an experience of heal-ing:

> In adoring Isaac, Abraham turns from God. The test, then, is an opportunity for understanding and healing. To relinquish attachment is to discover a glorious free-dom. To give up human anxiety is to receive divine as-surance. To disavow idolatry is to find God."[35]

Abraham was not Isaac's only parent, and Trible is not the only contemporary theologian to complain that the biblical story of Mount Moriah has omitted an important woman. We are left to imagine what Isaac's mother, Sarah, thought of the whole process. Did she even know what Abraham was up to that day? Trible regrets for Sarah that the mother who idolized the boy was not permitted to participate in the healing.

Some women who were the victims of incest or child abuse at the hands of their fathers suggest that no mother would ever take her child up that mountain as Abraham did. Yet every day in my clinic, I watch *Sarahs* lead their tearful children to the treatment room and hope that the first Sarah's good fortune will paral-lel their own. I know many mothers as well as fathers who have memorized the craggy rocks of Moriah's to-pography.

I have had many fathers who, in the moment of their child's own suffering, have been haunted by memories of the civilians they killed as soldiers in Vietnam. These men have come to mistrust their ability under pressure to be fully human for another human being. As often as I have heard about the My Lai massacre from fathers of that generation, I have also heard about contemplated or attempted abortions of this particular child's pregnancy from mothers. Other parents' stories may be less dramatic, but each *Sarah* and each *Abraham* brings the pages of their own human history to the base of that awful mountain as they ask, "Why me?" It is only the children on Moriah whose list of regrets makes short reading.

જ઼ જ઼ જ઼

Psychiatrist Scott Peck, who participated in the investigations of My Lai during the Vietnam War, warns that the tendency to avoid pain and suffering is "the primary basis of all human mental illness."[36] Perhaps this is why I can recall so many parents who have experienced unbelievable holocaust through loving a child with cancer but seem so mentally healthy. I once shared Peck's unusual definition with a pediatrician who is the son of an esteemed Orthodox Jewish scholar. He brooded for a moment, then reflected, "That's not a medical concept; that's a theological point of view."

God called out, "Abraham!" and the patriarch answered, "Here I am." We do not know Sarah's version of the story, but we do know about one of her descendants, generations later. When God's angel Gabriel called to an unwed pregnant teenager, Mary answered, like Abraham, "Here am I." In a recent talk to hospice volunteers, I reached for a suitable metaphor to impart something of the beauty of the mothers with whom I work. *I have met Mary many times.*

Time after time, I see young mothers who keep strange things and ponder them in their hearts, mystified women whose precocious children seem preoccupied with their Father's business. And yes, also the *pieta*—like Mary, they cradle the broken body of a great little miracle as they once had held a newborn in swaddling clothes. I have met Marys with many faces and marvel at their serenity and courage. Sarah's son survived, but Mary's Son became the lamb that God provided. You've suffered much, Mary, and you walked back down Calvary's hill alone, without your Son. But truly you are blessed amongst women. Through you, Sarah receives her healing.

꘠ ꘠ ꘠

It is another one of those gray days when I must set out for Moriah to meet my newest Sarah and Abraham and Isaac. I have set up a base camp at the foot of the mountain because I must return so often. There is a nice big rock at my camp that has become "my rock." The peak of the mount is wrapped in mist tonight, and there is an ominous wind starting to make its presence felt as I set myself down on my rock, looking up.

Moriah is not only treacherous but ugly. A few hundred yards ahead I see the bare reminder of the trail that was last pursued to the top. I have never seen undergrowth spring back as fast as on Moriah, making it more difficult for newcomers to find the previously blazed trail. The vegetation on Moriah seems to have germinated in Hades, implanting itself as mature brush when the winds blow it in. The thorn bushes here do not even bother with the mockery of berries. No one who comes here would be fooled anyway, and none can escape the nasty encounter by choosing an easier path.

Some other Abrahams and Sarahs and even Isaacs have come back from the peak to write their own trail guides. Some of them speak of the literary process as exorcism. You would have to share in a Moriah experience to fully understand the metaphor. These volumes line the shelves of my office and are well worn by pilgrims, but they seem almost useless the night before the journey. The ink seems temporarily to fade on the pages, as if to lower its voice to a respectful whisper.

I don't like the feel of the wind on my face tonight as I look to the distance for the little family. It is Abraham I see first, simply because the former marine is so tall and powerfully built that he cannot be missed. Ordinarily people smile ironically when they see him dwarf the tiny slip of a girl they call Sarah who is walking at his side. Child of a farm, Sarah's diminutive size disguises her strength.

As they come closer, I can see that although Abraham is carrying the supplies, it is Sarah who bears Isaac in her arms. She carried him for nine months in her body, and there is no way to prevent her from carrying him now. The child has not been able to walk for many months and despite his bulk, she carries him effortlessly.

A long time ago I indicated to her my amazement at her physical strength. She laughed and retorted that her daddy told her that if she picked up a calf on the day it was born and every day thereafter, by the time the beast was full grown, she might even be able to pick up the whole cow. I was never one to argue with the earthy wisdom of farmers.

Mother and father put down their burdens temporarily, and we plan the strategy for the ascent. Abraham puts his arm around Sarah tenderly to shield her from the frightful wind, and I imagine that I see their entire history as lovers flash in his eyes. In a single moment, he recalls and regrets each time he has treated her shabbily and undervalued one of the most admirable human beings he (and I) will ever be privileged to know. The intensity of his love is mirrored there as well. We have been through too much together for me to turn my eyes away as an embarrassed voyeur.

They understand that I can go no further with them. In our months and years together, I have only been able to train them in the tactics of a Moriah climb. The trail guide must remain below when the trek is finally made. I wait until Sarah has Isaac safely snuggled in her arms before I embrace them both. Her eyes are dry and her gaze is toward the mountain, but Abraham releases tears that have been held back since Vietnam as

I take him in my arms. When the pain of a lifetime has been safely spent, I nod and they depart.

I return to my rock to wait but find myself rudely blown from my familiar seat by an uncommon wind. I seek a sturdy tree branch to grasp as an avalanche of mighty rocks descends from the fog-drenched peak, breaking my own rock in pieces. Before the rumble ceases, there is no familiar rock in my "safe place," only rubble. I hold to my new shelter, the tree, and shake with the rocks. The tree comforts me as I had comforted Abraham.

Peace returns to the mountain but it is not long before I feel the first tremor beneath my feet. The tree shudders with me and the rocks quake once again. The tree and I cling to each other in terror wondering whether we will make it through the night. Neither the tree nor I have ever experienced an earthquake before. Ultimately, the ground settles and slowly we release our death grip on each other.

The thunder did not provide its usual early warning because of the other noises on the mountain tonight. No sooner have I released my hold on the tree than my friendly shelter is hit by lightning and consumed in fire. There seems to be no safe place to run to as other trees are blitzed and incinerated. The mountain burns like hell itself, and I am anxious for the small family negotiating its terrain. My impulse is to flee below to the safety of the city, but I remain and keep watch until the flames die out. There is only a charred corpse that remains of my tree.

No owl hoots. No chipmunk scurries. Even the wind has died. The silence that follows the wind, the earthquake, and fire are like the void that I imagine would follow a nuclear holocaust. Absolute silence. Then, softly, in the silence, comes a still small voice from the direction of Moriah's peak.

"Abraham?"

"Here am I, Lord!"

"Sarah, are you there, too?"

"Here I am, Lord!"

"Abraham, Sarah, I love you," the still small voice continues.

"Love us, Lord?" questions Abraham as he holds Sarah and Isaac to him.

"Sarah, whom I made to laugh because of Isaac. Abraham, the future father of many nations. Abraham! Sarah! Do you love me?"

❧ ❧ ❧

For Viktor, who placed his visa and manuscript on the altar, the question became not whether one escapes but rather *Shema Yisrael*. For Naomi, whose passion for motherhood was on the altar, the answer was not yes or no but God's love. Before Moriah, we think we know all the answers. On Moriah we learn that we did not even know what the question was.

— Epilogue —

Saying Amen

The Spirit and the bride say,
"Come." And let everyone who
hears say, "Come." And let
everyone who is thirsty come. . . .
The one who testifies to these things
says, "Surely I am coming soon."
Amen. Come, Lord Jesus!

Revelation 22:17, 20 (NRSV)

*S*ometimes I ask parents: "If you could rewrite the story of your life, would you wipe out this experience without any trace?" Although they would all omit the physical suffering of their child, few would want to return to their former philosophy of life. A mother once confided to me that until her own son developed leukemia, she had never thought about a single seriously ill child. In our hospital, her eyes were opened to the vast and varied problems that can afflict our young. Her child had leukemia, but there were these other children with heart failure, kidney disease, and chromosomal syndromes—organ failure, after disease, after syndrome. She could only conclude that either they had all been previously hidden in some closet or her own view of the world was too narrow and protected.

Charles Hummel comments,

> The book of Job . . . gives clues to the meaning of suffering. But we do not really understand this message—in fact, we hardly take it seriously—until we suffer. Our initial knowledge may come from the Bible, but

deeper understanding comes only as we put teaching into practice.[37]

❧ ❧ ❧

A father who lost three children in early infancy to the same miserable disease told me that he personally believed God was more than passively involved in their suffering as a family—belief more painful than unbelief. Yet at the emergency birth of their fourth child, realizing that once again they had lost, they postponed their own grief to organize the medical staff of a small community hospital. Thanks to them, blood samples, placenta, and autopsy material were preserved for a research team in a distant state. They facilitated a breakthrough in the understanding of the disease that will benefit children and parents of the future, but not them directly.

This couple may have lacked answers as to *why*, but they understood *what* action their faith required of them. Parents of children with cancer unite to support each other in organizations such as "Candlelighters."[38] I hear the voices of these parents echo when I read J. B. Phillips's rendering of 2 Corinthians 4:9: "We may be knocked down but we are never knocked out!"

❧ ❧ ❧

Eileen is another wonderful mother. She became so interested in the spiritual welfare of children after her own son was diagnosed with leukemia that she returned to graduate school for a degree in religious education. When her son's leukemia relapsed and he was admitted to the hospital, she used quiet moments while he slept to study. One day in his hospital room, I noticed some books written by theologians who are famous for their skeptical opinions about the miraculous stories in the Bible and I asked Eileen why she was reading those particular theologians.

"I'm taking a course entitled: 'Is the resurrection of Jesus Christ relevant today?'" I told her that I knew what those authors said about the Resurrection, but I was more interested in what she had to say. It was with great peace and joy that she looked at her seriously ill son who was laboring to breathe and answered, "I *know* that it's relevant!"

I write these words on Good Friday, one week after the death of Eileen's son. I am reminded that without the agony of the Cross, the Resurrection would have been just as irrelevant as some contemporary theologians believe it to be. It would be far easier to turn our backs on Jesus' cross and claim only his resurrection and triumph. But then we quickly lose the power of the very miracle we seek to celebrate, and we would be forgetting Jesus' words that we must take up our own crosses if we would follow him.

❧ ❧ ❧

My own vision of God is more informed by these "parental theologians" I meet in my clinic than the best and most brilliant scholars who rarely venture from the safety of their essays and books, pulpits and classrooms. David Biebel's first-born son died in early childhood from a bizarre neurological disease, and his second son is afflicted with the same rare syndrome. In a poem entitled "Lament" this evangelical pastor asks,

> Destroy! Destroy! Our little boy,
> What sad, demented mind, unkind
> Would dare?
> GOD?[39]

When his second son was diagnosed with the same illness, he dared to articulate what he was actually feeling: "If that's the way it's going to be, then God can go to hell!"

They were honest words, but they tasted like blasphemy on his tongue. As he drove to his parents' home that night to tell them that Christopher too was afflicted with the illness that took Jonathan's life, he realized the ironic truth of his "blasphemous" words and with that realization came God's comfort. On Good Friday, at the place of the skull, God *did* go to hell. As David sobbed, he sensed God's message to him: "I understand, my son. I've been there already. I've felt your pain and carried your sorrows. I know your words arose from grief beyond control and I love you still and always will."[40]

Let me return to my prayer for my young friend Tony. It was not an exercise of the head but a demand of the heart. My prayer, "Don't you care at all?" was answered in my heart as quickly as my thoughts blasted the heavens: "Yes, I do care and it's because I care that you are there. And I am there also."

Those in the fiery furnace find One who walks with them. Those who walk through the valley of the shadow of death do not walk alone. God, the Parent who so loved the world, became a co-sufferer with all parents who share Mount Moriah's supreme test of faith, through the gift and death of his beloved Son.

Before my career is complete, there will be many more Tonys to choke back their tears. I doubt that many of their parents will report that all of their hard theological questions found answers. Neither will I, and we continue to pose some awfully tough arguments.

At least when we challenge God, we keep a conversation going. That type of conversation is called prayer. And occasionally in the conversation, God interrupts, so to speak, and gets a word or two in edgewise. To hearts untroubled and hearts unsure, there is a window to heaven in the abiding promise that Jesus will come. *Amen. Come, Lord Jesus!*

Notes

1. Albert Camus, *The Plague*, translated by Stuart Gilbert (New York: Random House, 1965), 260.
2. Alan C. Mermann, "Coping Strategies of Selected Physicians," *Perspectives in Biology and Medicine* 33, no. 2 (1990): 2.
3. The modern hospice movement began in England with the work of Dr. Cicely Saunders at St. Christopher's Hospice in London. In the area of Connecticut where I work, home-care services are available to extend the same philosophy to terminally ill patients who wish to remain at home. Because of the special relationship that our child patients have to their pediatric nurses, we use our own inpatient unit to extend the hospice concept of care when home care is not the preferred option. The International Children's Hospice Program is an organization that seeks to promote the best care for children with terminal illnesses.
4. Let the record show that the AMA never banned house calls! That may be a historical fact, but an amazing number of lay people associate the disappearance of house calls with the political activity of this major physicians' organization.

5. Some names and events have been changed to protect privacy.

6. Dianne Klein, "The Visions of Dying Children Seem to Bring God Alive," *Los Angeles Times, Orange County Edition,* April 22, 1990.

7. Paul S. Minear, *John, the Martyr's Gospel* (Cleveland, Ohio: Pilgrim Press, 1984), 59.

8. Klein, "Visions of Dying Children."

9. Although I am not writing here about near-death experiences, such experiences have been recorded for children, many with spiritual content. In her book *Chasing the Dragon* (London: Hodder and Stoughton, 1980), Jackie Pullinger tells of a four-year-old Chinese boy who was pronounced dead after a drowning accident. He sat up after he was dressed for burial and told his mother of a man who held out his hand and pulled him out of the water. His mother asked him if he knew the man's name, assuming it was the headmaster of the school where the accident occurred. "Don't you know?" replied the boy. "It's Jesus." This family had fled from mainland China and had never had contact with Christians. His mother, who had never before heard the name of Jesus, became a Christian as a result of this child's near-death experience.

10. Henri J. M. Nouwen, *Letters to Marc about Jesus* (San Francisco: Harper & Row, 1987), 41.

11. Words and music by C. Austin Miles, Copyright 1912 by Hall-Mack Co.

12. See Minear, *John, the Martyr's Gospel,* 61.

13. Sophia Cavalletti, *The Religious Potential of the Child,* translated by Patricia M. and Julie M. Coulter (New York: Paulist Press, 1983).

14. Henry VanDyke, *The Story of the Other Wise Man* (New York: Harper & Row, 1895).

15. Jason Gaes, *My Book for Kids with Cansur* (Melius & Peterson, 1989), 42. Jason's parents and the editors of his book had the wisdom to preserve his spelling and grammar and I have followed their example.

16. Peter Kreeft, *Making Sense out of Suffering* (Ann Arbor: Servant Books, 1986).

17. The syndrome was first described in 1866 by John Langdon Down, medical superintendent of the Earlswood Asylum for Idiots in Surrey, England, in an article entitled, "Observations on an Ethnic Classification of Idiots." Influenced by Darwinism, he theorized that the slanted eyes were a throwback to Mongolian origins. The term "Mongolian idiot" is inappropriate as well as offensive, and the term "Down's syndrome" is to be preferred.

18. An editorial in the *American Journal of Psychiatry* (99: p. 141) in 1942 argued, "The state of mind of the parents of an idiot may fairly become a subject of psychiatric concern . . . fear of opinion even deters sometimes from placing a mentally deficient child in an institution when the interests of the child and family alike would best be served by such action."

19. Such advice was given to Dale Evans and Roy Rogers when their Down's daughter, Robin, was born in 1950. When Dale published her book, *Angel Unaware* (Old Tappan, NJ: Revell, 1953) she took the world by surprise and gave courage to other parents who chose to keep their retarded children in the bosom of the family.

20. "*Les petite bouffonnes du bon Dieu*" (God's little clowns) is applied to Down's syndrome by Morris West

in his wonderful novel, *The Clowns of God* (New York: William Morrow, N. Y. 1981), 336.

21. Author's translation of German praise song. Copyright 1972 by Peter Janssens Music Publishers, 4404 Telgte, West Germany.

22. Feminist theologian Susan Nelson Dunfee presents this position in her book, *Beyond Servanthood: Christianity and the Liberation of Women* (Lanham, Md.: University Press of America, 1989).

23. Wolf Wolfensberger, "The Prophetic Voice and Presence of Mentally Retarded People in the World Today," an edited presentation to the Religion Subdivision of the American Association of Mental Deficiency at its 100th national conference, Chicago, May 1976.

24. "The Poignant Thoughts of Down's Children Are Given Voice," *New York Times*, December 22, 1987.

25. Used with the permission of the family.

26. Henri J. M. Nouwen, *Reaching Out; The Three Movements of the Spiritual Life* (New York: Doubleday, 1975), 67, 68.

27. Richard C. Mouw, *Distorted Truth* (San Francisco: Harper & Row, 1989), 18.

28. A. J. Solnit, *The Noncustodial Father—An Application of Solomonic Wisdom, in Fathers and Their Families*, ed. Stanley H. Cath, Alan Gurwit, and Linda Gunsberg (Hillsdale, N.J.: Analytic Press, 1989).

29. Kyle Pruett, author of *The Nurturing Father* (New York: Warner, 1987), has studied fathers as primary parents and the impact of their special style of nurturing on subsequent child development.

30. William F. May, *The Patient's Ordeal* (Bloomington: University of Indiana Press, 1991).

31. Elie Wiesel, *Messengers of God* (New York: Random House, 1976), 74.
32. As interviewed on Robert Schuller's television program, "Hour of Power," August 18, 1991.
33. Viktor Frankl, *Psychotherapy and Existentialism* (New York: Simon and Schuster, 1967), 119.
34. Viktor Frankl, *Psychotherapy and Existentialism*, 25.
35. Phyllis Trible, "Genesis 22: The Sacrifice of Sarah," Gross Memorial Lecture, Valparaiso University, Valparaiso, Indiana, 1989.
36. M. Scott Peck, *A Road Less Traveled* (New York: Simon and Schuster, 1978), 17.
37. Charles Hummel, *Fire in the Fireplace* (Downers Grove, Ill.: InterVarsity Press, 1978), 89.
38. Candlelighters is an international organization of parents of children with cancer. The name is taken from the motto, "It is better to light one candle than to curse the darkness."
39. David B. Biebel, *If God Is So Good, Why Do I Hurt So Bad?* (Colorado Springs: NavPress, 1989), 18.
40. Ibid.